Distribution and Joint Fish-Tag Survival of Juvenile Chinook Salmon Migrating through the Sacramento-San Joaquin River Delta, California, 2008

By Christopher M. Holbrook, Russell W. Perry, and Noah S. Adams

Prepared in cooperation with the Technical Committee of the Vernalis Adaptive Management Plan and the San Joaquin River Group Authority

Open-File Report 2009–1204

U.S. Department of the Interior
U.S. Geological Survey

U.S. Department of the Interior
KEN SALAZAR, Secretary

U.S. Geological Survey
Suzette M. Kimball, Acting Director

U.S. Geological Survey, Reston, Virginia: 2009

For more information on the USGS—the Federal source for science about the Earth, its natural and living resources, natural hazards, and the environment, visit http://www.usgs.gov or call 1-888-ASK-USGS.

For an overview of USGS information products, including maps, imagery, and publications, visit http://www.usgs.gov/pubprod

To order this and other USGS information products, visit http://store.usgs.gov

Suggested citation:
Holbrook, C.M., Perry, R.W., and Adams, N.S., 2009, Distribution and joint fish-tag survival of juvenile Chinook salmon migrating through the Sacramento-San Joaquin River Delta, California, 2008: U.S. Geological Survey Open-File Report 2009-1204, 30 p.

Contents

Abstract 1

Introduction 2

Methods 4

    Data Collection 4

        Fish Handling, Tagging, and Release 4

        Acoustic Receivers 5

        Evaluating Tag Failure 5

    Data Analyses 6

        Travel Times 6

        Estimating Survival and Migration Route Probabilities 6

        Parameter Estimation 8

        Population-Level Parameters 9

        Model Selection 10

Results 11

    Tag Failure 11

    Travel Times 11

    Fish-Tag Survival and Migration Route Probabilities 14

    Fish-Tag Survival for Fish That Traveled through Old River 15

    Fish-Tag Survival for Fish That Traveled through San Joaquin River and Turner Cut 15

    Entrainment of Tagged Fish into Old River 16

Discussion 16

    Entrainment into Old River 16

    Fish-Tag Survival through the Delta 20

    Migration through the Central Delta 21

    Migration Past the Stockton Wastewater Treatment Plant 22

Summary 22

Acknowledgments 23

References Cited 24

Appendix A. Parameter definitions and estimates 27

Figures

Figure 1. Schematic of the San Joaquin River and Sacramento-San Joaquin Delta with acoustic monitoring and release sites used in the 2008 VAMP study 3

Figure 2. Schematic of release-recapture model used to estimate joint fish-tag survival (σ_{hi}), detection (P_{hi}), route entrainment (Ψ_{hl}), and transition ($\varphi_{hi,gj}$) probabilities for acoustically tagged juvenile Chinook salmon released in the San Joaquin River, California, 2008 7

Figure 3. (A) Empirical tag survival curve (solid black line; $N_0 = 66$) with theoretical 95-percent confidence interval (± 1.96 binomial SE) from the tag failure evaluation; and (B) travel time distributions, by release week, for tagged fish from release at Durham Ferry to first detection at: (1) the Old River-San Joaquin River junction (sites OLD, SJO.n); (2) the Turner Cut-San Joaquin River junction (sites TRN, SJT); (3) the State and Federal pumping projects, including the Clifton Court Forebay (sites SWP, CVP, CCFB); (4) Jersey Point or Threemile Slough (sites JPT, TMS); and (5) Chipps Island (site MAL) 12

Figure 4. Travel times from release at Durham Ferry to arrival at Chipps Island for tagged fish that traveled through the San Joaquin River (Route A; n = 16) and Old River (Route B; n = 15) 13

Figure 5. (A) Discharge in the San Joaquin River downstream of the Old River-San Joaquin River junction (dashed blue line) and in Old River (solid red line); with (B) fraction of San Joaquin River discharge flowing into Old River (solid black line) and cumulative arrival distributions at the Old River-San Joaquin River junction for tagged fish released in week 2 at Durham Ferry during the day (solid green line) and night (dashed blue line) 17

Figure 6. (A) Arrival distribution at the Old River-San Joaquin River junction and (B) proportion of tagged fish (with 95-percent binomial confidence interval) entrained into Old River as a function of the fraction of San Joaquin River discharge flowing into Old River at the time of arrival for fish released at Durham Ferry in week 2 18

Tables

Table 1. Release group, date, site, time of day, sample size, median fork length, and median weight of tagged juvenile Chinook salmon released into the San Joaquin River, California, 2008 4

Table 2. Total number of tagged juvenile Chinook salmon detected at five locations in the Delta, with proportion that arrived during day and night. 13

Table 3. Population-level parameter estimates (standard errors in parentheses) with 95-percent profile likelihood confidence intervals (C.I.) for tagged juvenile Chinook salmon released in weeks 1 and 2. 14

Conversion Factors

Inch/Pound to SI

Multiply	By	To obtain
Flow rate		
cubic foot per second (ft^3/s)	0.02832	cubic meter per second (m^3/s)

SI to Inch/Pound

Multiply	By	To obtain
Length		
millimeter (mm)	0.03937	inch (in.)
meter (m)	3.281	foot (ft)
kilometer (km)	0.6214	mile (mi)
Area		
square kilometer (km^2)	247.1	acre
Mass		
gram (g)	0.03527	ounce, avoirdupois (oz)

Temperature in degrees Celsius (°C) may be converted to degrees Fahrenheit (°F) as follows:
°F=(1.8×°C)+32

Concentrations of chemical constituents in water are given either in milligrams per liter (mg/L) or micrograms per liter (µg/L).

Distribution and Joint Fish-Tag Survival of Juvenile Chinook Salmon Migrating through the Sacramento-San Joaquin River Delta, California, 2008

By Christopher M. Holbrook, Russell W. Perry, and Noah S. Adams

Abstract

Acoustic telemetry was used to obtain the movement histories of 915 juvenile fall-run Chinook salmon (*Oncorhynchus tshawytscha*) through the lower San Joaquin River and Sacramento-San Joaquin Delta, California, in 2008. Data were analyzed within a release-recapture framework to estimate survival, route distribution, and detection probabilities among three migration pathways through the Delta. The pathways included the primary route through the San Joaquin River and two less direct routes (Old River and Turner Cut). Strong inferences about survival were limited by premature tag failure, but estimates of fish distribution among migration routes should be unaffected by tag failure. Based on tag failure tests (N = 66 tags), we estimated that only 55–78 percent of the tags used in this study were still functioning when the last fish was detected exiting the study area 15 days after release. Due to premature tag failure, our "survival" estimates represent the joint probability that both the tag and fish survived, not just survival of fish. Low estimates of fish-tag survival could have been caused by fish mortality or fish travel times that exceeded the life of the tag, but we were unable to differentiate between the two. Fish-tag survival through the Delta (from Durham Ferry to Chipps Island by all routes) ranged from 0.05 ± 0.01 (SE) to 0.06 ± 0.01 between the two weekly release groups. Among the three migration routes, fish that remained in the San Joaquin River exhibited the highest joint fish-tag survival (0.09 ± 0.02) in both weeks, but only 22–33 percent of tagged fish used this route, depending on the week of release. Only 4–10 percent (depending on week) of tagged fish traveled through Turner Cut, but no tagged fish that used this route were detected exiting the Delta. Most fish (63–68 percent, depending on week of release) migrated through Old River, but fish-tag survival through this route (0.05 ± 0.01) was only about one-half that of fish that remained in the San Joaquin River. Once tagged fish entered Old River, only fish collected at two large water conveyance projects and transported through the Delta by truck were detected exiting the Delta, suggesting that this route was the only successful migration pathway for fish that entered Old River. The rate of entrainment of tagged juvenile salmon into Old River was similar to the fraction of San Joaquin River discharge flowing into Old River, which averaged 63 percent but varied tidally and ranged from 33 to 100 percent daily. Although improvements in transmitter battery life are clearly needed, this information will help guide the development of future research and monitoring efforts in this system.

Introduction

Chinook salmon (*Oncorhynchus tshawytscha*) in California's Central Valley were decimated in the 19th and 20th centuries by overfishing, dam construction, channelization, pollution, and water diversions (Clark, 1929; Skinner, 1962, Yoshiyama and others, 1998; Williams, 2006). Of the four distinct runs (winter, spring, fall, late fall) present in the Central Valley, the winter and spring runs are listed as endangered and threatened, respectively, while populations of fall-run Chinook salmon remain the most abundant (Myers and others, 1998; Lindley and others, 2004). However, escapement of fall-run salmon recently decreased below minimum conservation targets, reaffirming the need for fundamental changes in fisheries and water management in the Central Valley (Healey and others, 2008; Lindley and others, 2009).

The San Joaquin River drains about 83,000 km^2 in California's Central Valley, and along with the Sacramento River, is a primary source of freshwater to San Francisco Bay. Lack of recovery of salmon populations in the San Joaquin River has been attributed to diversions and water storage dams that reduce river discharge during the spring runoff, when juvenile fall-run salmon are actively migrating (The Bay Institute, 2003; Williams, 2006). Flows in the lower San Joaquin River are regulated by upstream dams and exports from two water conveyance systems: the State Water Project and Central Valley Project. These projects are economically and socially important, as they provide water to more than 23 million residents and 3 million acres of agricultural land (Healey and others, 2008). Both projects divert water directly from Old River (fig. 1). At times, these facilities export all San Joaquin River water (Kimmerer, 2002). Reduced water velocities, altered water distribution, increased water temperatures, and reduced turbidity can increase mortality of juvenile salmonids through increased exposure to predators and greater susceptibility to diseases (Ferguson, 1981; Baker and others, 1995; Smith and others, 2003; Marine and Cech, 2004). Fish that arrive at these pumping projects are either entrained into water conveyance pumps or screened and collected (that is, "salvaged") at the fish collection facilities. Salvaged fish are then trucked and released into the western Delta near Jersey Point (fig. 1; site JPT). Although the export facilities are known to reduce San Joaquin River flows and cause direct mortality at the pumps (Kimmerer, 2008), mark-recapture experiments using coded wire tags have failed to detect a significant relation between export rates and survival of juvenile salmon (Newman and Rice, 2002; Newman, 2008).

Current management strategies aim to improve survival of juvenile salmon migrating from the San Joaquin River through the Sacramento-San Joaquin River Delta (hereafter, "the Delta") by augmenting San Joaquin River discharge and curtailing water exports in the spring (San Joaquin River Group Authority, 2009). These management actions have been conducted under the auspices of the Vernalis Adaptive Management Plan (VAMP), a long-term research program that was established to quantify the effects of alternative management actions on juvenile salmon survival. This report presents findings from research on the emigration and survival of juvenile salmon conducted under VAMP management actions during spring 2008. During this period, San Joaquin River flows were augmented by releases at upstream dams and curtailed exports at the pumping projects (for details, see San Joaquin River Group Authority, 2009). In previous years, a barrier was installed at the head of Old River to reduce the number of juvenile salmon exposed to the water pumping projects; but no barrier was installed in 2008.

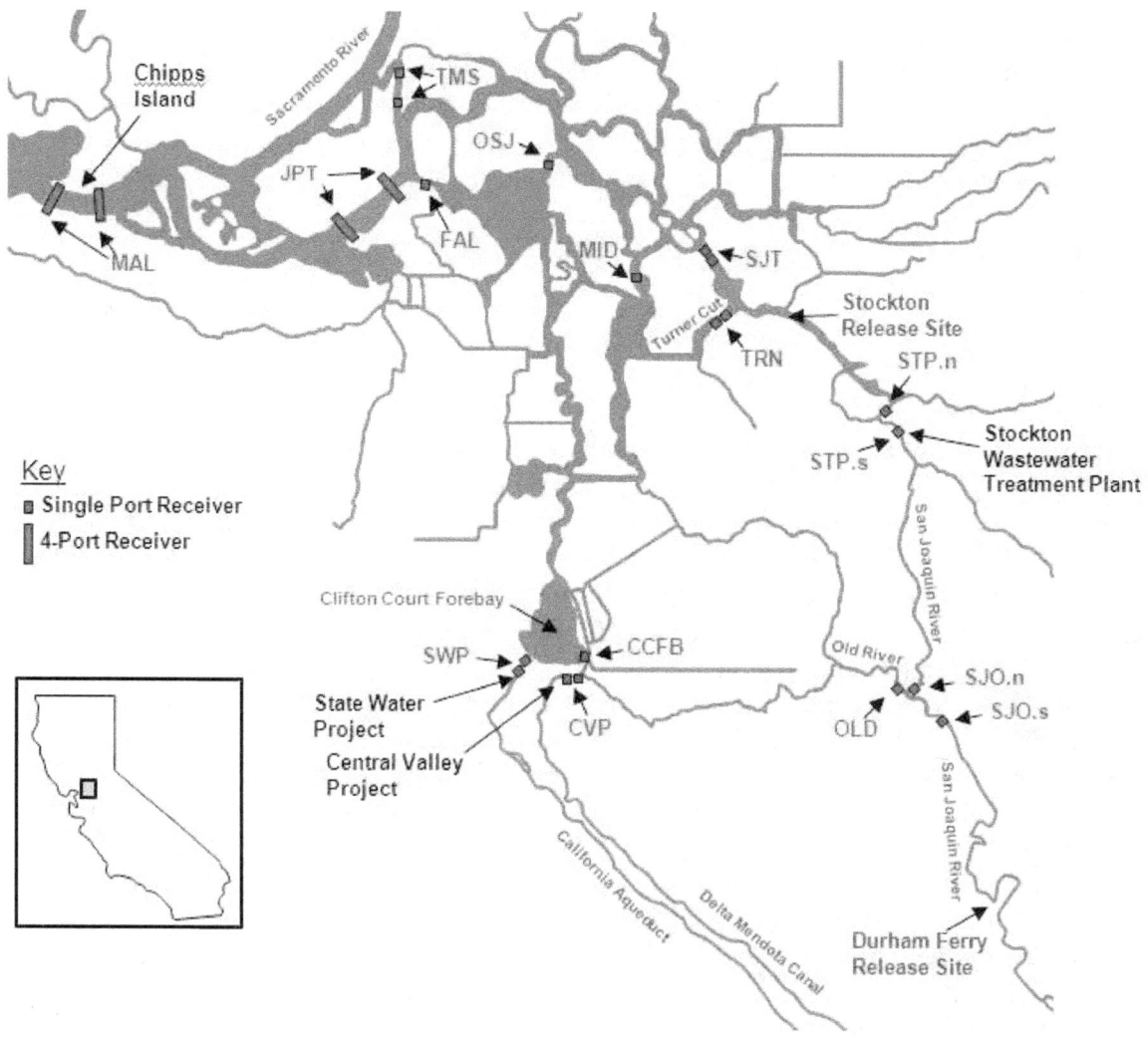

Figure 1. Schematic of the San Joaquin River and Sacramento-San Joaquin Delta with acoustic monitoring and release sites used in the 2008 VAMP study. The number of "ports" represents the number of hydrophones at each site.

The goals of this study were to: (1) estimate route- and reach-specific survival of juvenile Chinook salmon migrating from the San Joaquin River through the Delta by each of three pathways: the mainstem San Joaquin River (Route A), Old River (Route B), and Turner Cut (Route C); (2) quantify route entrainment probabilities at two junctions where fish leave the San Joaquin River and enter two alternative migration routes (routes B and C); and (3) describe travel times through the study area. Acoustic telemetry was used to obtain movement histories for emigrating juvenile Chinook salmon at 16 locations between release in the San Joaquin River at Durham Ferry (river km, rkm, 112) and exit from the Delta at Chipps Island (fig. 1), including the entrance to Clifton Court Forebay (fig. 1; site CCFB) and the intakes at the State Water and Central Valley Projects. Recently, acoustic telemetry techniques have been selected over coded wire tags for use in VAMP research due to the very low capture probabilities of coded wire tags (median capture probability ≤ 0.0008 at the Chipps Island trawl; Newman, 2008) and the inability to estimate the proportion of fish using different migration routes with coded wire tags. In contrast, acoustic telemetry data can be analyzed within a release-recapture framework to provide maximum likelihood estimates of survival, route entrainment, and detection probabilities with better precision than coded wire tags.

Methods

Data Collection

Fish Handling, Tagging, and Release

Yearling, fall-run Chinook salmon were obtained from the California Department of Fish and Game's Merced River Hatchery in Snelling, Calif. Fish were anesthetized in a buffered (70 mg/L NaHCO$_3$) tricane methanosulfonate (70 mg/L) solution, their fork length and weight were recorded (table 1), and then acoustic tags (model 795-S; Hydroacoustic Technology, Inc., HTI, Seattle, Wash.) were implanted according to procedures outlined by Adams and others (1998) and Martinelli and others (1998). The tags were 16.4 mm long, 6.7 mm in diameter, and weighed 0.65 g in air, representing 4.3 percent of the mean fish weight (range = 2.3–5.8 percent). Each tag emitted a unique double-pulsed acoustic signal (2 ms pulse width) every 8.6–10.0 s and had an expected minimum battery life of 11 days. After tagging, fish were held for about 18 h, transported to the release site, and released after being acclimated for 1–3 h in river water. Further details on the tagging and release procedures are provided by San Joaquin River Group Authority (2009).

In total, 915 fish were tagged and released (table 1). Releases were divided equally between two release periods (weeks 1 and 2), separated by 7 days. Fish were released into the San Joaquin River at Durham Ferry and at Windmill Cove (rkm 57) near Stockton (fig. 1). Within each release period, about 60 percent of the fish were released at Durham Ferry and 40 percent were released at Stockton. On each release day, about one-half of the fish were released during the day and one-half were released at night.

Table 1. Release group, date, site, time of day, sample size, median fork length, and median weight of tagged juvenile Chinook salmon released into the San Joaquin River, California, 2008.

[Ranges are given in parentheses]

Release period	Date	Release site	Time	Number of samples	Median fork length, in millimeters	Median weight, in grams
Week 1	April 29	Durham Ferry	Day	144	109 (103–120)	14.9 (12.1–21.2)
			Night	138	110 (101–125)	15.1 (12.1–22.8)
	May 1	Stockton	Day	93	108 (100–117)	14.6 (12.3–20.0)
			Night	94	109 (102–123)	14.5 (12.1–25.4)
Week 2	May 6	Durham Ferry	Day	139	108 (100–122)	14.1 (12.1–20.8)
			Night	144	111 (103–132)	15.6 (11.8–28.7)
	May 8	Stockton	Day	85	112 (103–123)	15.3 (12.3–21.8)
			Night	78	110 (102–130)	15.0 (12.1–24.8)

4

Acoustic Receivers

Tagged fish were detected in holding tanks at the Merced River Hatchery before transport and release. Movements of tagged fish through the study area were monitored by autonomous receivers at 16 sites between Durham Ferry and Chipps Island (fig. 1). Fourteen sites were monitored using single-hydrophone acoustic receivers (HTI model 295). Due to the width of the channel at Jersey Point (site JPT) and Chipps Island (site MAL), receivers with four hydrophones (HTI model 291) were used to ensure complete "bank-to-bank" coverage as tagged fish passed these locations. All single-hydrophone receivers were maintained by Natural Resource Scientists, Inc. (Red Bluff, Calif.). The U.S. Geological Survey (California Water Science Center, Sacramento, Calif.) maintained receivers at Jersey Point and Chipps Island. Duplicate receivers were installed at seven sites (MAL, JPT, TMS, SJT, TRN, SWP, and CVP) to estimate detection probabilities (see section, "Estimating Survival and Migration Route Probabilities"). Quantifying detection probabilities using duplicate receivers was particularly important at Chipps Island, where survival and detection probabilities would have otherwise been confounded because there were no detection sites downstream of Chipps Island. Detections at three sites (MID, OSJ, FAL) provided behavioral information, but were not included in the release-recapture model because they lacked double detection arrays necessary to estimate detection probabilities.

Acoustic receivers were operated for 24 days after the last fish was released. Detections recorded by the receivers were initially identified using an auto-detection routine in the software program MarkTags (HTI) and then further validated by visually examining echograms of potential detections (Ehrenberg and Steig, 2003).

Evaluating Tag Failure

One major assumption of using acoustic tags to estimate survival is that all surviving fish exit the study area (that is, pass Chipps Island) with functioning tags. Premature tag failure, defined as failure of any tag before a live fish passes Chipps Island, will negatively bias survival estimates (that is, true survival will be greater than estimated survival) because release-recapture models will interpret tag failure as fish mortality. We tested 66 tags in a closed system to quantify the rate of tag failure over time. Tags were continuously monitored with an acoustic telemetry receiver (HTI model 290) in a water-filled tank until all tags ceased to operate. Because water temperature affects the life expectancy of the tag, we controlled water temperature in the tank (ranged from 15 to 21°C during the study period) to mimic the daily mean water temperature in the San Joaquin River at Jersey Point (data obtained from http://cdec.water.ca.gov/; accessed April 2009). The time-to-failure of each tag was calculated as the elapsed time between initiation and final detection. We constructed an empirical cumulative distribution function from the time-to-failure data to estimate the probability that any tag survived to a given date.

Data Analyses

Travel Times

The travel time for each tagged fish between release and any downstream monitoring site was calculated as the elapsed time between release and first detection at the downstream site. Individual travel times were calculated from release to (1) the Old River-San Joaquin River junction (sites SJO and OLD); (2) the Turner Cut-San Joaquin River junction (sites SJT and TRN); (3) water export facilities (sites CCFB, SWP, and CVP, collectively); (4) Jersey Point and Threemile Slough (sites JPT and TMS); and (5) Chipps Island (site MAL). We present plots of travel time distributions and differences in median travel times (D_M) between various groups (for example, weeks 1 and 2, routes A and B). Due to tag failure, the true median travel times probably are longer than we observed. We did not test for travel time differences among weeks or sites because travel times, like fish survival estimates, are negatively biased due to premature tag failure.

Estimating Survival and Migration Route Probabilities

Following the framework presented by Perry and others (in press), we developed a multi-state release-recapture model to estimate detection (P_{hi}), route entrainment (Ψ_{hl}), survival (S_{hi}), and transition probabilities ($\varphi_{hi,gj}$; see Brownie and others, 1993 and Skalski and others, 2002). The full model (fig. 2) consisted of 3 migration routes (A, B, C), 2 groups (Durham Ferry, Stockton), and 68 parameters: 2 tag survival probabilities, 16 joint fish-tag survival probabilities, 2 route entrainment probabilities, 20 transition probabilities, and 28 detection probabilities (see appendix A, table A1 for parameter definitions). Detection probabilities (P_{hi}) estimate the probability that a tagged fish is detected at site h_i (h = a, b, c, d, e) given that the fish survives to site h_i with an operational tag. Route entrainment probabilities (Ψ_{hl}) estimate the probability of a fish entering channel h at junction l (l= 1, 2) given that the fish survives to junction l. Survival probabilities (S_{hi}) estimate the probability that a tagged fish survives from site h_i to the next downstream site.

A branching process was used to model entrainment probabilities into Old River and Turner Cut. At the first junction (Old River-San Joaquin River junction), Ψ_{a1} estimates the probability that a fish remains in the San Joaquin River. Conversely, $\Psi_{b1} = (1- \Psi_{a1})$ estimates the probability that a fish is entrained into Old River at this location. At the second junction (Turner Cut-San Joaquin River junction), Ψ_{a2} estimates the probability of a fish remaining in the San Joaquin River, and $\Psi_{c2} = (1- \Psi_{a2})$ estimates the probability that a fish is entrained into Turner Cut at this location.

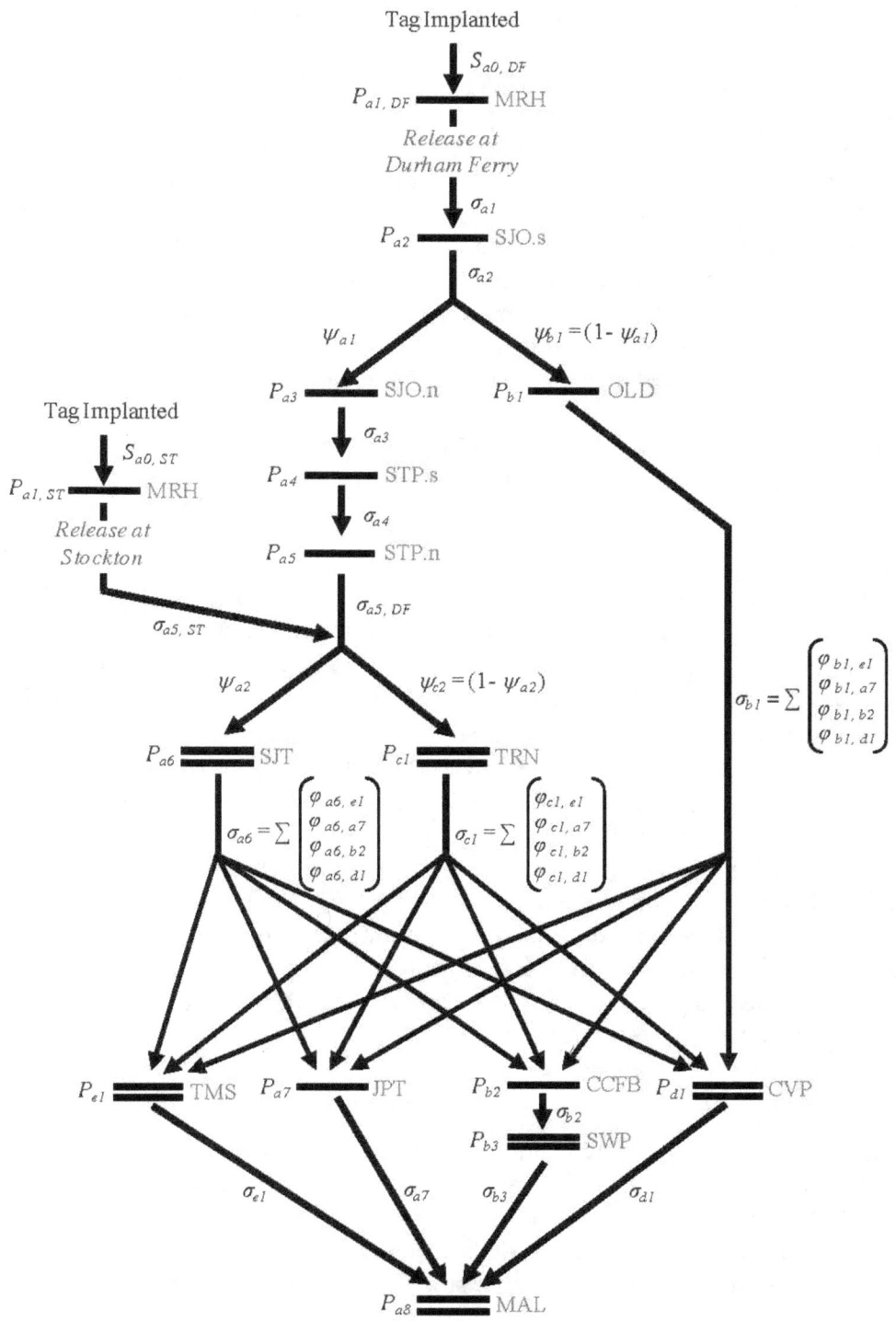

Figure 2. Schematic of release-recapture model used to estimate joint fish-tag survival (σ_{hi}), detection (P_{hi}), route entrainment (Ψ_{hi}), and transition ($\varphi_{hi,gj}$) probabilities for acoustically tagged juvenile Chinook salmon released in the San Joaquin River, California, 2008. Horizontal bars represent detection stations.

In the lower Delta, fish could exit some reaches at multiple locations by taking different migration pathways through unmonitored river junctions. In these situations, it is impossible to estimate separately the probability of taking each pathway from the probability of survival in a particular pathway. Thus, transition probabilities ($\varphi_{hi,gj}$) estimate the joint probability of surviving between h_i and g_j and taking a migration pathway connecting site h_i to g_j. Although biological interpretation of an individual $\varphi_{hi,gj}$ is difficult, the sum of all $\varphi_{hi,gj}$ over all exit locations (g_j) for a given h_i yields the probability of survival from site h_i to all possible exit sites from this reach (Brownie and others, 1993). Parameter estimates will be unbiased if all model assumptions are satisfied (Burnham and others, 1987; Skalski and others, 2002). The tag failure trial was specifically designed to test the assumption that each tag remained operational during migration of fish through the study area. However, results from the tag failure trial revealed that this assumption was not satisfied (see section, "Results"), yielding negatively biased estimates of S_{hi}.

When tag failure (or tag loss) is present in mark-recapture data, each estimate of survival actually represents the combined probability of tag "survival" and fish survival:

$$\sigma_{hi} = S_{hi,\text{tag}} S_{hi,\text{fish}}$$

$$(1)$$

Where $S_{hi,tag}$ and $S_{hi,fish}$ are the survival probabilities for the tag and the fish, and σ_{hi} is the joint probability that both the tag and fish survive from site h_i to the next downstream site. Eqn. 1 shows that only when $S_{hi,tag} = 1$ (that is, zero probability of tag failure) will $\sigma_{hi} = S_{hi,fish}$, providing an unbiased estimate of fish survival. Because we estimated that $S_{hi,tag} < 1$ in this study, we report σ_{hi} to explicitly indicate that these estimates represent the joint probability of both fish and tag survival (hereafter, "fish-tag survival"). Although a low estimate of σ_{hi} can not be interpreted as low fish survival alone, it does indicate some combination of fish mortality and travel times that exceeded the life of the tag.

One novel aspect of this model is that detections in holding tanks at Merced River Hatchery (site MRH) were included in the detection history, which allows estimation of P_{a1}, the detection probability in holding tanks during the hour prior to transport, and S_{a0}, the probability of tag survival between implantation and release. In essence, S_{a0} estimates the proportion of functioning tags at release and prevents bias associated with tag failure in the hatchery from estimates of in-river survival in the first reach.

Parameter Estimation

We used maximum likelihood techniques to estimate parameters based on a multinomial probability model that categorized each fish into a mutually exclusive and exhaustive detection history. Perry and others (in press) provide a concise explanation of the detection histories used in this type of model. There were 1,400 possible unique detection histories for fish released at Durham Ferry and 84 possible unique detection histories for fish released at Stockton. Each detection history represents one cell of a multinomial distribution where the probability of each cell is defined as a function of the detection, fish-tag survival, route entrainment, and transition probabilities (for details, see Perry and others, in press).

Given the cell probabilities, the maximum likelihood estimates are found by maximizing the likelihood function of a multinomial distribution with respect to the parameters:

$$L_{km}\left(\underset{\sim}{\beta}\middle| R_{km}, n_{jkm}\right) \propto \prod_{j=1}^{J} \pi_{jkm}^{n_{jkm}}$$

(2)

where L_{km} is the likelihood for the kth release group (k = week 1, week 2) at the mth release site (m = Durham Ferry (DF), Stockton (ST)), R is the number of fish released, n_j is the number of fish with the jth detection history, and π_j is the probability of the jth detection history expressed as a function of the parameters ($\underset{\sim}{\beta}$). Auxiliary likelihoods were used to estimate the detection probabilities at the double-detection array at Chipps Island, as described by Skalski and others (2002). Auxiliary likelihoods were not used to estimate detection probabilities at other double-detection sites because detection histories indicated that detection probabilities at these and many other sites were equal to 1.0 (see appendix A, table A2). Similarly, transition and fish-tag survival probabilities were set to 0 or 1 where appropriate. The likelihood was numerically maximized with respect to the parameters using the software program USER (Lady and others, 2008). Parameters were estimated separately for each release week (k) but simultaneously for both release sites (m) by expressing the joint likelihood as the product of $L_{k,DF}$ and $L_{k,ST}$. We examined Anscombe residuals (McCullah and Nelder, 1983) to assess goodness of fit for each full model.

Population-Level Parameters

Population-level parameters were estimated as combinations of reach- and route-specific parameters estimated by the model. Migration route probabilities (Ψ_r) represent the probability that any tagged fish used migration route r (r = A, B, C), and were estimated as functions of route entrainment probabilities:

$$\Psi_A = \Psi_{a1}\Psi_{a2};$$

(3)

$$\Psi_B = (1 - \Psi_{a1}) = \Psi_{b1}; \text{ and}$$

(4)

$$\Psi_C = \Psi_{a1}(1 - \Psi_{a2}) = \Psi_{a1}\Psi_{c2}.$$

(5)

Route survival probabilities (σ_r) represent the probability that a tagged fish survived with a functioning tag from Durham Ferry to Chipps Island, given that it entered route r. When route entrainment probabilities are estimated at every junction, fish-tag survival between Durham Ferry and Chipps Island is simply the product of all survival probabilities that trace each migration path through the Delta (Perry and others, in press). However, when the model includes transition probabilities ($\varphi_{hi,gj}$) survival through each migration path must account for all possible pathways where transition probabilities are estimated. Thus, fish-tag survival probabilities were derived for each route as:

$$\sigma_A = \sigma_{a1}\sigma_{a2}\sigma_{a3}\sigma_{a4}\sigma_{a5}\left(\varphi_{a6,e1}\sigma_{e1} + \varphi_{a6,a7}\sigma_{a7} + \varphi_{a6,b2}\sigma_{b2}\sigma_{b3} + \varphi_{a6,d1}\sigma_{d1}\right);$$

(6)

$$\sigma_B = \sigma_{a1}\sigma_{a2}\left(\varphi_{b1,e1}\sigma_{e1} + \varphi_{b1,a7}\sigma_{a7} + \varphi_{b1,b2}\sigma_{b2}\sigma_{b3} + \varphi_{b1,d1}\sigma_{d1}\right); \text{ and}$$

(7)

$$\sigma_C = \sigma_{a1}\sigma_{a2}\sigma_{a3}\sigma_{a4}\sigma_{a5}\left(\varphi_{c1,e1}\sigma_{e1} + \varphi_{c1,a7}\sigma_{a7} + \varphi_{c1,b2}\sigma_{b2}\sigma_{b3} + \varphi_{c1,d1}\sigma_{d1}\right).$$

(8)

9

Total fish-tag survival through the Delta among all routes (σ_{Delta}) was calculated as the sum of fish-tag survival among all routes, weighted by each migration route probability:

$$\sigma_{Delta} = \Psi_A \sigma_A + \Psi_B \sigma_B + \Psi_C \sigma_C. \tag{9}$$

We used the "Delta" method (Seber, 1982) to estimate the standard error for derived parameters. Profile likelihood 95-percent confidence intervals also were estimated (appendix A, table A2).

Model Selection

Releases at Stockton were intended to supplement sample sizes in the lower mainstem San Joaquin River. Ideally, detection, survival, route entrainment, and transition probabilities could be pooled between the two releases to increase precision of each parameter estimate. Pooling among releases, however, assumes that survival and route entrainment probabilities are equal between fish released at each site. Therefore, we used Akaike's information criterion (AIC) to test whether parameters could be assumed equal between release sites (Burnham and Anderson, 2002). Among candidate models, the model with the smallest AIC value represents the model with the most favorable tradeoff between precision and accuracy of the estimates (that is, over-fitting versus under-fitting). The difference in AIC values (Δ_{AIC}) between two models represents the degree of support for one model over another (Burnham and Anderson, 2002). As a general rule, $\Delta_{AIC} < 2$ indicates little or no evidence that either model is more appropriate than the other model. Thus, when $\Delta_{AIC} \geq 2$, we selected the model with the smallest AIC value, but when $\Delta_{AIC} < 2$, we selected the model with the fewest number of parameters. We selected the model with the fewest parameters when $\Delta_{AIC} < 2$ in order to simplify presentation of the results with the assumption that this would have minimal affect on resulting estimates.

Three candidate models were developed for each release period. Under the full model (Model 1: $P_{im}\sigma_{im}\Psi_{im}\varphi_{im}$), all parameters were estimated separately for each monitoring site i and release site m. In the first reduced model, each detection probability was set equal between the two release sites (Model 2: $P_i \cdot \sigma_{im}\Psi_{im}\varphi_{im}$). If Model 2 was selected over Model 1, then each detection, fish-tag survival, route entrainment, and transition probability was set equal between the two release sites in the final candidate model (Model 3: $P_i \cdot \sigma_i \cdot \Psi_i \cdot \varphi_i \cdot$). If Model 1 was selected over Model 2, then all detection probabilities were estimated separately in the final model, but each fish-tag survival, route entrainment, and transition probability was set equal between the two release sites (Model 3: $P_{im}\sigma_i \cdot \Psi_i \cdot \varphi_i \cdot$). We never set S_{a0} or P_{a1} equal between release sites because these parameters were not used to estimate population-level parameters. We never set σ_5 equal between release sites because the Stockton release site was located within this reach. For the same reason, all population-level parameters, where appropriate, were estimated with $\sigma_{5, DF}$ and never with $\sigma_{5, ST}$.

Results

Tag Failure

All test tags in the extinction trial expired within 20 days of initialization (fig. 3A; see San Joaquin River Group Authority, 2009). Test tags showed steady failure of about 2 percent per day between days 1 and 15, followed by rapid expiration between days 15 and 20. The estimated probability of tag survival to the start of day 12 (that is, expected minimum tag life) was 0.79 ± 0.05 (binomial SE). We estimate that 55–78 percent (95-percent confidence interval) of the tags were still functioning when the last fish was detected at Chipps Island, 15 days after release.

Travel Times

Tagged fish predominantly arrived at monitoring sites during daylight (table 2). Most tagged fish reached the Old River-San Joaquin River junction within 1.5 days after release at Durham Ferry (fig. 3B), but took 2–8 days after release to reach the Turner Cut-San Joaquin River junction. Tagged fish reached the pumping facilities faster than they reached the Turner Cut-San Joaquin River junction ($D_M = 1.76$ days). Fish reached Jersey Point ($D_M = 2.95$ days) and Chipps Island ($D_M = 2.81$ days) faster after release in week 2 compared to week 1, but much smaller differences were observed between weeks at the Old River-San Joaquin River junction ($D_M = 0.03$ days) and the pumping facilities ($D_M = 0.08$ days).

Fish released at Durham Ferry arrived at Chipps Island 2.9–14.9 days (median 8.8 days) after release in week 1, and 2.5–11.3 days (median 5.6 days) after release in week 2. Fish released at Stockton arrived at Chipps Island 5.6–11.3 days (median 8.3 days) after release during week 1, and 3.3–13.3 days (median 5.3 days) after release during week 2. Although sample sizes were small, tagged fish that traveled through Old River (Route B) reached Chipps Island (by salvage and trucking) faster than fish that traveled through the mainstem San Joaquin River past both junctions (Route A; fig. 4; $D_M = 3.68$ d). Travel times were not available for tagged fish that traveled through Turner Cut (Route C) because none of the 49 tagged fish detected in this route were detected at Chipps Island.

11

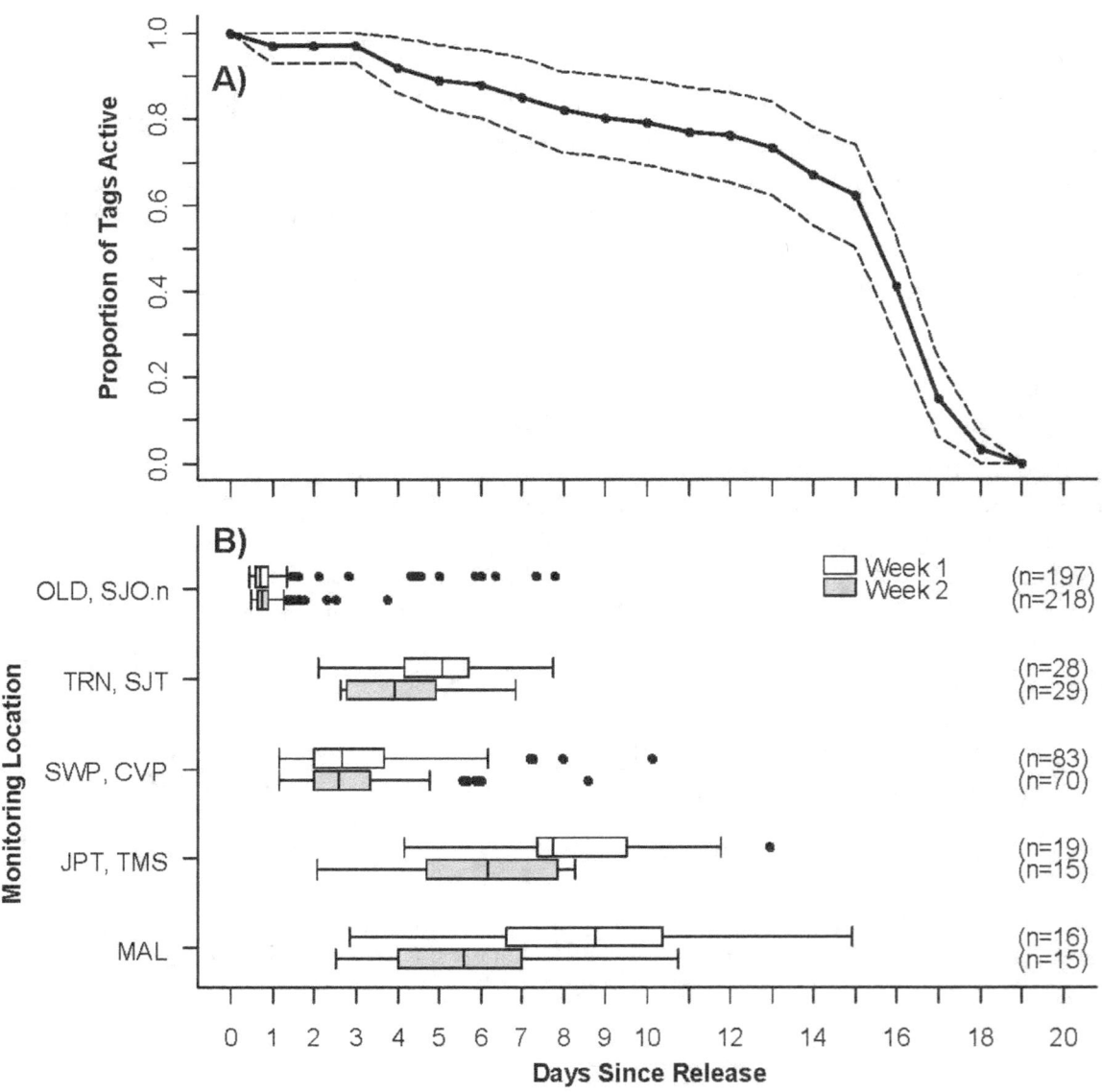

Figure 3. (A) Empirical tag survival curve (solid black line; $N_0 = 66$) with theoretical 95-percent confidence interval (±1.96 binomial SE) from the tag failure evaluation; and (B) travel time distributions, by release week, for tagged fish from release at Durham Ferry to first detection at: (1) the Old River-San Joaquin River junction (sites OLD, SJO.n); (2) the Turner Cut-San Joaquin River junction (sites TRN, SJT); (3) the State and Federal pumping projects, including the Clifton Court Forebay (sites SWP, CVP, CCFB); (4) Jersey Point or Threemile Slough (sites JPT, TMS); and (5) Chipps Island (site MAL). Sample sizes (numbers of fish detected) are shown at right. Box shows median, 25th and 75th percentiles. Whiskers extend to 1.5 times the interquartile range. Symbols show observations greater than 1.5 times the interquartile range.

Table 2. Total number of tagged juvenile Chinook salmon detected at five locations in the Delta, with proportion that arrived during day and night.

[Daylight was defined as the period between morning and evening civil twilights at Stockton, Calif., for each day. Daily civil twilight data were obtained from <http://www.usno.navy.mil/>.]

Release site(s)	Monitoring location	Monitoring sites	Total number	Percentage of day	Percentage of night
Durham Ferry	Old R.-San Joaquin R. Junction	OLD SJO	415	94.2	5.8
Durham Ferry	Turner Cut-San Joaquin R. Junction	TRN SJT	57	82.5	17.5
Stockton	Turner Cut-San Joaquin R. Junction	TRN SJT	212	76.0	24.0
Durham Ferry	Water Pumping Facilities	SWP CCFB CVP	153	71.9	28.1
Durham Ferry and Stockton	Chipps Island	MAL	72	86.1	13.9

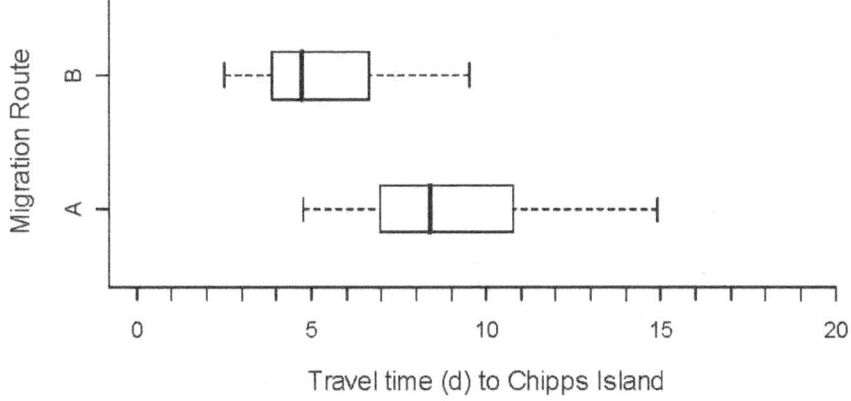

Figure 4. Travel times from release at Durham Ferry to arrival at Chipps Island for tagged fish that traveled through the San Joaquin River (Route A; n = 16) and Old River (Route B; n = 15). Route C is not shown due to insufficient data (n = 0). Box shows median, 25th and 75th percentiles. Whiskers extend to minimum and maximum.

Fish-Tag Survival and Migration Route Probabilities

We found little evidence of overdispersion (that is, greater variability in the data than expected under the model), as only 1 of the 2,980 encounter history frequencies (across both weeks) was more extreme than expected given the fitted model estimates (that is, the absolute value of the Anscombe residual was greater than 1.96). Although the residual for the encounter history was 2.71, only two individuals were observed with this history for which 0.15 individuals were expected. For week 1, the AIC values were 283.0, 278.3, and 279.1 for models 1 ($P_{im}\sigma_{im}\Psi_{im}\varphi_{im}$), 2 ($P_i\cdot\sigma_{im}\Psi_{im}\varphi_{im}$), and 3 ($P_i\cdot\sigma_i\cdot\Psi_i\cdot\varphi_i\cdot$), respectively. Among these, we selected Model 3 because $\Delta_{AIC} = 0.8$ and Model 3 had the fewest parameters (29 versus 32). For week 2, the AIC values were 200.00, 203.4, and 198.3 for models 1 ($P_{im}\sigma_{im}\Psi_{im}\varphi_{im}$), 2 ($P_i\cdot\sigma_{im}\Psi_{im}\varphi_{im}$), and 3 ($P_{im}\sigma_i\cdot\Psi_i\cdot\varphi_i\cdot$), respectively. Among these, we selected Model 3 because it had the smallest AIC value and fewest parameters (29 versus 32). Note that the selected model (Model 3) differs between the 2 weeks. Although fish-tag survival and route entrainment probabilities were set equal between release sites for both weeks, we set all detection probabilities equal between release groups in week 1, but not week 2.

Fish-tag survival probabilities through the Delta (σ_{Delta}) were 0.06 ± 0.01 (SE) and 0.05 ± 0.01 for weeks 1 and 2, respectively (table 3). Most tagged fish traveled through Old River (Route B; $\Psi_B = 0.68$ and 0.63 in weeks 1 and 2, respectively) and were salvaged and trucked. Fewer fish traveled through the San Joaquin River (Route A) past both junctions ($\Psi_A = 0.22$ and 0.33), and a small proportion of the fish traveled through Turner Cut (Route C; $\Psi_C = 0.10$ and 0.04). Fish-tag survivals for each route were consistent between weeks (table 3) and were highest for Route A ($\sigma_A = 0.09 \pm 0.01$), lower for Route B ($\sigma_B = 0.05 \pm 0.02$), and lowest for Route C ($\sigma_C = 0.00$).

Table 3. Population-level parameter estimates (standard errors in parentheses) with 95-percent profile likelihood confidence intervals (C.I.) for tagged juvenile Chinook salmon released in weeks 1 and 2.

	Week 1		Week 2	
Parameter	Estimate (SE)	95% C. I.	Estimate (SE)	95% C. I.
σ_{Delta}	0.053 (0.013)	0.032, 0.082	0.061 (0.012)	0.040, 0.089
σ_A	0.094 (0.024)	0.056, 0.149	0.092 (0.019)	0.059, 0.135
σ_B	0.048 (0.017)	0.022, 0.088	0.048 (0.017)	0.022, 0.088
σ_C	0.001 (0.001)	0.000, 0.005	0.000	
Ψ_A	0.215 (0.029)	0.162, 0.277	0.333 (0.032)	0.274, 0.397
Ψ_B	0.681 (0.038)	0.605, 0.752	0.625 (0.034)	0.558, 0.689
Ψ_C	0.103 (0.019)	0.071, 0.145	0.041 (0.011)	0.023, 0.067

Fish-Tag Survival for Fish That Traveled through Old River

Within Route B, fish-tag survival was lowest through the three reaches associated with the pumping projects: the Clifton Court Forebay ($\sigma_{b2} = 0.37 \pm 0.09$ and 0.39 ± 0.10 for weeks 1 and 2); the State Water Project ($\sigma_{b3} = 0.16 \pm 0.10$ and 0.47 ± 0.15); and the Central Valley Project ($\sigma_{b2} = 0.11 \pm 0.05$ and 0.05 ± 0.04). Estimated transition probabilities from Old River to Jersey Point (site JPT) and Threemile Slough ($\varphi_{b1,e1}$ and $\varphi_{b1,a7}$) were not greater than 0.01 for either week (appendix A, table A2), indicating that tagged fish that traveled through Old River either exclusively reached Chipps Island (that is, exited the Delta) through the collection facilities at the pumping projects (including transport) or that none of the fish that traveled through Old River traversed the central Delta with a functioning tag. Of all tagged fish detected in Old River (site OLD; Route B), only 2 percent (4 of 187) were later detected at the secondary sites (1 at MID, 3 at FAL).

Fish-Tag Survival for Fish That Traveled through San Joaquin River and Turner Cut

Routes A and C have three reaches in common between the Old River and Turner Cut junctions (figs. 1 and 2). Among these, fish-tag survival was lowest in the reach between site STP.n and the Turner Cut-San Joaquin River junction ($\sigma_{a5, DF} = 0.49 \pm 0.07$ and 0.56 ± 0.07 for weeks 1 and 2). Although similar in size, fish-tag survival was higher (compared to $\sigma_{a5, DF}$) in the reach that extended from the Old River-San Joaquin River junction to site STP.s ($\sigma_{a3} = 0.85 \pm 0.05$ and 0.70 ± 0.05). Estimated fish-tag survival through the reach containing the Stockton Wastewater Treatment Plant (σ_{a4}) were 0.96 ± 0.03 in week 1 and 0.89 ± 0.05 in week 2 (appendix A, table A2).

Lower fish-tag survival for Route C ($\sigma_C = 0.00$) compared to Route A ($\sigma_A = 0.09$) can be attributed to low fish-tag survival ($\sigma_{c1} = 0.03 \pm 0.03$ and 0.00 for weeks 1 and 2) between the entrance to Turner Cut and any of the next monitoring sites (JPT, TMS, CCFB, SWP, or CVP). Similarly, of all tagged fish detected in Turner Cut (site TRN; Route C), only 4 percent (2 of 49; both at site MID) were later detected at any of the three sites that were not included in the release-recapture model.

For fish that survived to the junction of Turner Cut, the estimated probabilities of entrainment into Turner Cut were 0.32 ± 0.05 for week 1 and 0.11 ± 0.03 for week 2. Thus, most tagged fish remained in the San Joaquin River at its junction with Turner Cut. Transition probabilities from the San Joaquin River near Turner Cut to the pumping projects ($\varphi_{a6,d1}$ and $\varphi_{a6,b2}$) were zero, indicating that tagged fish that traveled through Route A did not enter routes leading to the pumping projects, or that none of the tagged fish that used this route traversed the central Delta with a functioning tag. However, of all fish detected in the San Joaquin River below its junction with Turner Cut (site SJT; Route A) 22 percent (40 of 186; 24 at MID, 6 at OSJ, 10 at FAL) were later detected at the three sites that were not included in the release-recapture model. This suggests that some fish that traveled through Route A entered the central Delta, but none reached the pumping projects alive or with a functioning tag.

Entrainment of Tagged Fish into Old River

Old River discharge was inversely related to discharge in the San Joaquin River downstream of the Old River-San Joaquin River junction (fig. 5A). The mean fraction of San Joaquin River discharge flowing into Old River at the Old River-San Joaquin River junction was 63 percent between April 29 and May 13, 2008 (that is, the period when tagged fish arrived at this location) and ranged from 33 to 100 percent. During the strongest flood tide each day, 100 percent of the San Joaquin River discharge flowed into Old River (fig. 5B). During this time, the San Joaquin River flow reversed direction downstream of the head of Old River, but maintained constant downstream flow upstream of the head of Old River. As little as 33 percent of the San Joaquin River discharge flowed into Old River during the strongest ebb tide each day. Most tagged fish arrived at the head of Old River when flows were either 40–50 percent or 90–100% (figs. 5 and 6A). Although the flow distribution was bimodal over the fish arrival distribution, the proportion of tagged fish entrained into Old River (Route B) was similar to the fraction of the San Joaquin River discharge flowing into Old River at the time of arrival (fig. 6B).

Discussion

Although unbiased estimates of fish survival could not be obtained, this study succeeded in estimating many important components of migration dynamics that would have been difficult to measure using other methods (for example, coded wire tags). For example, most juvenile salmon traveled through Old River and were entrained into Old River at a rate similar to the fraction of San Joaquin River discharge flowing into Old River. Unlike fish survival estimates, entrainment and migration route probabilities obtained from these data are unlikely to be biased. Despite wide flow variation within each day, flow dynamics were similar among days throughout the study (see San Joaquin River Group Authority, 2009). Thus, estimates of entrainment and migration route probabilities probably were not affected by either long travel times or tag failures.

Entrainment into Old River

It is widely hypothesized that fish are distributed among routes at a junction in proportion to the fraction of water flowing into each route. Indeed, the fraction of San Joaquin River discharge flowing into Old River during the study period (63 percent) was very similar to the overall proportion of fish that were entrained into Old River (68 and 63 percent for weeks 1 and 2; appendix A, table A2). However, the fraction of San Joaquin River discharge flowing into Old River was highly variable within each day, ranging from 33 to 100 percent (fig. 5B). We were unable to model (for example, with logistic regression) the proportion of fish entrained into Old River as a continuous function of discharge flowing into Old River because the fish arrival distribution occurred over a very limited range of the flow distribution and detection probabilities were less than 1.0 at this location. Most fish arrived when either 40–50 percent or 90–100 percent of the San Joaquin River discharge was flowing into Old River (fig. 6A). Still, these data show that most tagged fish were entrained into Old River at a rate similar to the fraction of San Joaquin River discharge that flowed into Old River when each fish arrived at the junction (fig. 6B).

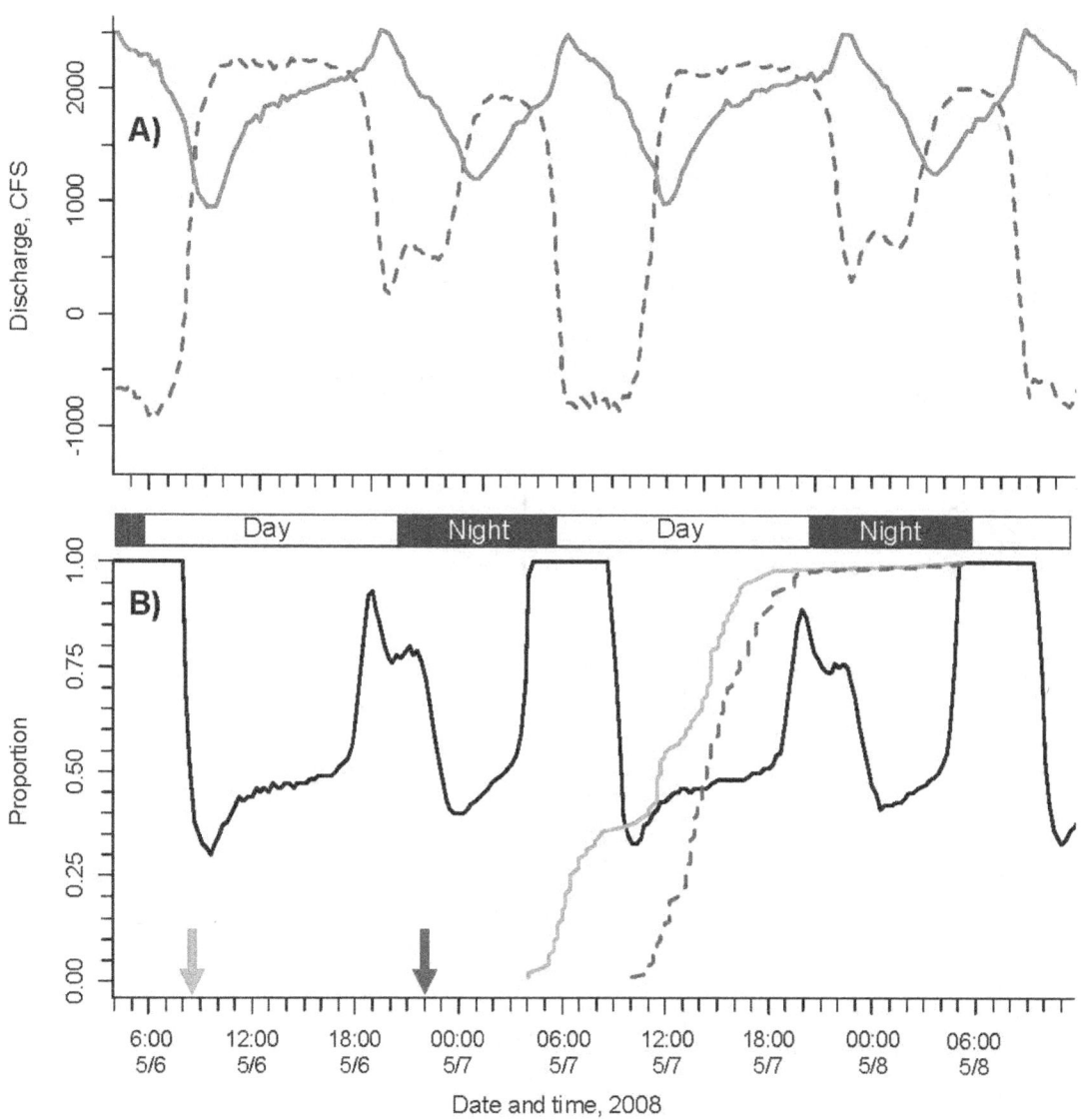

Figure 5. (A) Discharge in the San Joaquin River downstream of the Old River-San Joaquin River junction (dashed blue line) and in Old River (solid red line); with (B) fraction of San Joaquin River discharge flowing into Old River (solid black line) and cumulative arrival distributions at the Old River-San Joaquin River junction for tagged fish released in week 2 at Durham Ferry during the day (solid green line) and night (dashed blue line). Arrows indicate date and time of release at Durham Ferry during the day and night. Discharge data were obtained from <http://cdec.water.ca.gov/>. Old River discharge was measured at CDEC station OH1, located in Old River about 250 m downstream of the Old River-San Joaquin River junction. Total San Joaquin River discharge at the Old River-San Joaquin River junction was estimated as the sum of discharge at OH1 and in the San Joaquin River near Lathrop (CDEC station SJL; located about 450 m downstream of the Old River-San Joaquin River junction).

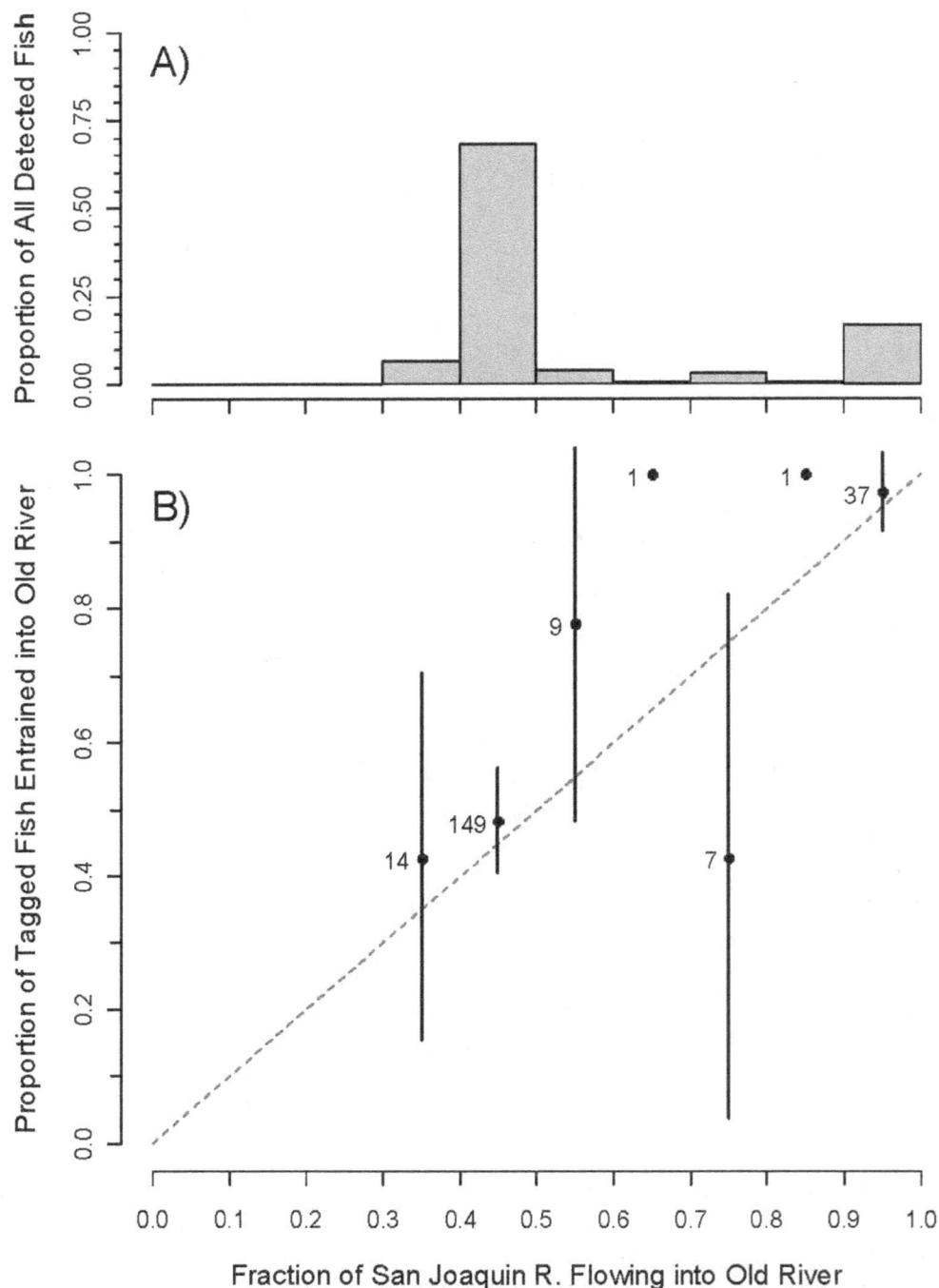

Figure 6. (A) Arrival distribution at the Old River-San Joaquin River junction and (B) proportion of tagged fish (with 95-percent binomial confidence interval) entrained into Old River as a function of the fraction of San Joaquin River discharge flowing into Old River at the time of arrival for fish released at Durham Ferry in week 2. The reference line shows where the proportion of fish entrained is equal to the fraction of San Joaquin River discharge flowing into Old River. Sample sizes are given for each data point.

The "as-measured" discharge was used in these analyses, not the tidally averaged discharge that is most commonly used in a management context. Thus, time of arrival of fish in the junction with respect to tidal current phase, as it is mediated by export operations, is important in determining entrainment of juvenile salmon into Old River. In lieu of a barrier (physical or non-physical), an effective way to prevent fish from entering Old River may be to minimize exports at specific times to reduce the proportion of the San Joaquin River discharge flowing into Old River when most juvenile salmon are arriving at the Old River-San Joaquin River junction (for example, during the day and possibly during flood tides). Changes in exports would need to be timed so that desired changes in flows at the head of Old River would occur at desired times. The appropriate timing (for example, how long it takes for a change in Clifton Court operations to change flows at the head of Old River) and magnitude of the changes could be deduced from modeling studies and tested in the field using the existing flow station network.

In previous years, a physical barrier was installed into the head of Old River to minimize entrainment of juvenile salmon into the State and Federal pumping projects. Previous studies showed that the barrier improved survival of juvenile salmon migrating through the San Joaquin River (Brandes and McLain, 2001). However, because the physical barrier reduced the discharge in Old River, it was considered a threat to the endangered Delta smelt (*Hypomesus transpacificus*) and its installation was prohibited starting in 2008. Although physical barriers are no longer permitted, non-physical barriers are currently being tested at this site (P. Brandes, U.S. Fish and Wildlife Service, oral commun., 2009). Consistent with previous studies (San Joaquin River Group Authority, 2008) tagged fish in this study arrived at the Old River-San Joaquin River junction almost exclusively during the day (table 2). Future barriers may only need to be effective during the day at this time of year to deter most juvenile salmon from entering Old River. Managers should consider, however, that diel activity patterns in juvenile salmon are known to change in response to varying environmental conditions (see Wilder and Ingram, 2006, and references therein).

It also is important to recognize that release timing may have influenced when fish arrived at the Old River-San Joaquin River junction in this study. The narrow range of arrival times (fig. 3B) suggests that release timing may have affected arrival timing at this location and could have resulted in observed behaviors that are not representative of the run-of-river population. For example, many fish released during the day in week 2 arrived at the Old River-San Joaquin River junction when 100 percent of San Joaquin River discharge was flowing into Old River, but none of the fish that were released at night arrived during this condition (fig. 5B). To best represent arrival times of the untagged population, future studies may benefit from an intermittent release strategy, where fish are released in smaller groups throughout the day and night, rather than in a few discrete bulk releases. Releasing fish farther upstream also may result in more "natural" behavior as tagged fish approach the Delta.

Episodic failures of acoustic monitoring equipment also can affect the ability to assess fish entrainment relative to other factors, such as the proportion of San Joaquin River discharge flowing into Old River at the Old River-San Joaquin River junction. For example, when a receiver is not operating properly in one route at a junction, but continues to function in the other route, analyses that quantify the relation between a covariate (for example, proportional flow) and the probability of entrainment when each fish arrives at a junction are not appropriate because one route is underrepresented in the data (that is, $P < 1.0$). This was the case during week 1, when detection probabilities were low in Route B ($P_{b1} = 0.47$) but high in Route A ($P_{a3} = 0.98$) at the Old River-River San Joaquin River junction. The detection probability in Route B was higher ($P_{b1} = 0.94$) during week 2 than week 1. Thus, we only included fish released in week 2 in our analysis of entrainment into Old River as a function of the fraction of San Joaquin River discharge flowing into Old River.

Fish-Tag Survival through the Delta

This study also highlights the importance of study-specific tag failure data to explicitly test for premature tag failure. In the absence of tag failure data, one must assume that tag failure does not occur prior to fish exiting the study region. In this study, fish survival would have been underestimated had we not explicitly assessed this assumption. Corrections for bias due to tag failure exist (Cowan and Schwarz, 2005. Townsend and others, 2006) but assume that the estimated travel time distribution is unbiased. Because the travel time distribution also is negatively biased due to tag failure in this study, we could not adjust the survival estimates to account for tag failure and do not advocate management actions based solely on the results of this study. Nonetheless, the fish-tag survival probabilities obtained in this study are informative, as low estimates indicate either mortality or travel times that exceeded the life of the tag.

Fish-tag survival through the Delta was consistent among weeks ($\sigma_{Delta} = 0.05$ and 0.06; table 3), but much lower than survival reported by Perry and others (in press) for tagged Sacramento River juvenile salmon migrating through the Delta. Among the three routes, fish that traveled through the San Joaquin River (Route A) past the first two junctions showed the highest fish-tag survival ($\sigma_A = 0.09$ in both weeks), but only 22–33 percent of the study population used this route (Ψ_A) among weeks. Conversely, most of the fish (63–68 percent range between weeks) traveled through Old River (Ψ_B), where estimated fish-tag survival ($\sigma_B = 0.05$) was about one-half that of Route A. Only 4 and 10 percent of tagged fish traveled through Turner Cut (Ψ_B) in weeks 1 and 2, but no fish using this route were detected downstream ($\sigma_C = 0.00$) in either week. Such heterogeneity in survival and distribution among only three major migration routes reiterates the need to obtain a population-level understanding of distribution and survival through this spatially complex and hydraulically dynamic system.

Comparisons of reach-specific estimates (appendix A, table A2) reveal that differences in fish-tag survival between routes A and C (highest and lowest fish-tag survival) can be attributed to the reaches represented by the parameters σ_{a6} and σ_{c1} (see fig. 2). These estimates indicate that 44 and 50 percent (weeks 1 and 2) of all tagged fish that arrived at the Turner Cut-San Joaquin River junction and proceeded through the San Joaquin River, survived with a functioning tag (σ_{a6}) to another monitoring site (for example, Jersey Point, Three-Mile Slough, or the pumping facilities). In contrast, 0 and 3 percent (weeks 1 and 2) of the tagged fish that entered Turner Cut at this junction survived with a functioning tag (σ_{c1}) to another monitoring site. These findings indicate that fish entering Turner Cut either died or were delayed (relative to Route A) to the extent that their tags failed before exiting the Delta.

A similar comparison of reach-specific estimates between routes A and B (San Joaquin River and Old River) reveals that the difference in fish-tag survival between these routes are probably *not* attributable to the reaches represented by parameters σ_{a6} and σ_{b1}. Despite lower fish-tag survival in Route B compared to Route A, and although σ_{b1} represents fish-tag survival over a greater distance (for example, analogous to $\sigma_{a3}\sigma_{a4}\sigma_{a5}\sigma_{a6}$ for Route A), 51–65 percent (between weeks) of tagged fish that entered Old River survived with a functioning tag (σ_{b1}) to another site. Rather, the data show that low fish-tag survival through the Clifton Court Forebay (σ_{b2}; appendix A, table A2) and between the intake at each of the pumping facilities and Chipps Island (σ_{b3} and σ_{d1}) account for lower fish-tag survival through Old River compared to the San Joaquin River. Of all tagged fish that arrived at Clifton Court Forebay, we estimated that 37 and 39 percent (weeks 1 and 2) survived with a functioning tag to the intakes of the State Water Project. Of those fish that arrived at the intakes of the State Water Project, we estimated that 16 and 47 percent (weeks 1 and 2) exited the Delta with a functioning tag. Of those fish that arrived at the Central Valley Project, we estimated that 5 and 11 percent (weeks 1 and 2) exited the Delta with a functioning tag. In comparison, we estimated that 61 and 71 percent (weeks 1 and 2) of fish that reached Jersey Point exited the Delta with a functioning tag (σ_{a7}). Although confidence intervals around these estimates are large (see appendix A, table A2), these results suggest that successful passage through the Delta through Old River is most limited by low survival or delays in reaches containing the Clifton Court Forebay, State Water Project, and Central Valley Project.

Migration through the Central Delta

"Successful" migration (defined as $\sigma_r > 0$) was observed in only two of the three pathways that were monitored. No tagged fish that entered Turner Cut were detected at Chipps Island. Salvage at the pumping facilities and subsequent transport also seemed to be the only successful migration pathway for tagged fish that traveled through Old River. The opposite was true of fish that traveled through the San Joaquin River past Turner Cut—successful migrants exclusively traveled past Jersey Point or Threemile Slough, rather than through the pumping projects. Detections at the three monitoring sites (MID, OSJ, FAL) that were excluded from the release-recapture model also support these observations. Of all tagged fish detected in Old River, only 2 percent were detected at any of these three sites, and one-half of those fish were detected at site FAL after salvage at the Central Valley Project, transport, and release into the western Delta.

Fish that traveled through Old River also reached Chipps Island faster than fish that traveled through the San Joaquin River (fig. 4), although travel times were only available for fish that survived this reach and were detected at Chipps Island. Fish may have traveled faster through Old River because unlike fish that traveled through other routes, they experienced no reversing flows prior to salvage, transport, and release into the western Delta.

Of all tagged fish detected in Turner Cut, only 4 percent were detected at any of the three sites that were not included in the release-recapture model. Although detection probabilities were not estimable at any of the three sites excluded from the model, 21 percent (40 of 186) of tagged fish known to use Route A were detected in these channels (sites MID, OSJ, FAL), but only one of these was detected at the Clifton Court Forebay or either pumping project. These results, along with the very low apparent success of migrants that traveled through Turner Cut ($\sigma_{c1} \leq 0.03$) provide evidence that conditions in the central Delta impose either mortality or long travel times (exceeding tag life of 2–20 days) on nearly all migrants that travel through the central Delta.

Migration Past the Stockton Wastewater Treatment Plant

In 2007, the San Joaquin River Group Authority (2009) observed that 116 of 776 tags released in the San Joaquin River were found "not moving" near the Stockton Wastewater Treatment Plant. Based on these observations, it was suspected that high mortality in this region might have been caused by degraded water quality from treatment plant effluent. In this study, fish-tag survival probabilities were relatively high (ranged 0.89 to 0.96 between weeks) through the reach containing the treatment plant. Based on our point estimates of fish-tag survival, we predict that about 8 of the 565 fish that were released upstream of the treatment plant and remained in the San Joaquin River past its junction with Old River, would have died in this reach. Because of the large difference between years, it seems reasonable to assume that mortality in this reach was lower in 2008 than in 2007.

As a result of the suspected high mortality that was identified during the 2007 study, the San Joaquin River Group Authority (2009) monitored water quality and survival in this reach during 2008. Water-quality monitoring indicated that ammonia concentrations did not exceed U.S. Environmental Protection Agency standards during the study period. To evaluate fish survival, fish implanted with non-functioning tags were held in the river near the effluent of the wastewater treatment plant, but no mortalities or sub-lethal effects were observed.

Summary

Perry and others (in press) illustrated the importance of estimating both route entrainment and survival probabilities in order to gain an understanding of population-level survival during juvenile salmon migration through a complex system like the Delta. Compared to traditional mark-recapture techniques (for example, releases of coded wire tagged fish) acoustic telemetry provides greater temporal and spatial detail about the outmigration process. Further, continuous, simultaneous monitoring at several locations allows estimation of entrainment probabilities at river junctions and reach- and route-specific survival throughout the study region. If premature tag failure can be reduced to a negligible rate, future studies that use telemetry techniques should be able to address many important management questions, including the objectives of the VAMP. The rates of premature failure observed in this study were not observed in other studies using similar tags from the same manufacturer (Adams and others, 2008; Adams and Counihan, 2009) and were thus unexpected. In response to these results, the manufacturer has discontinued the tag model used in this study (795-S) and has re-designed their products to minimize the occurrence of premature tag failure in future studies (B. Ransom, HTI, oral commun., 2008).

Although the joint fish-tag survival probabilities reported in this study may be of limited use to fishery and water resource managers, these data suggest that either high mortality or long travel times (relative to other routes) are prevalent among juvenile salmon migrating through the central Delta. Further, these results support the hypothesis that in the absence of a barrier at the head of Old River, the proportion of juvenile salmon traveling through Old River is similar to the fraction of San Joaquin River discharge flowing into Old River. There remains great potential to further understand the relations among discharge, water exports, and survival of migrating salmon through the San Joaquin River and Sacramento-San Joaquin Delta. Although complete answers to these questions will require replication over several years and a variety of conditions (for example, barrier placements, discharge, export operations), results from this study illustrate that these objectives are attainable. Recent advancements in acoustic telemetry technology, along with quantitative analytical approaches, should soon provide managers with much-needed data for salmon and water management in this system.

Acknowledgments

This work was funded under Interagency Agreement no. 08AA200078 with the U. S. Bureau of Reclamation with financial support provided by the U.S. Bureau of Reclamation, U.S. Fish and Wildlife Service, California Department of Water Resources, California Department of Fish and Game, San Joaquin River Group Authority, State Water Contractors and the San Luis and Delta-Mendota Water Authority. We thank P. Brandes (U.S. Fish and Wildlife Service) for managing the study; T. Liedtke (USGS Columbia River Research Laboratory) and A. Fuller (FishBio Environmental) for fish tagging and release; Dave Vogel (Natural Resource Scientists, Inc.), Jon Burau and Aaron Blake (USGS California Water Science Center) for installing and operating acoustic receivers; and Jon Burau and John Beeman (USGS Columbia River Research Laboratory) for reviewing this report. We also thank S. Brewer, S. Foott, J. Ingram, J. Lewis, M. Marshall, K. Nichols, P. Hrodey, B. Powell, J. Speegle, R. Stone, J. Thompson, C. Vallee, P. Voong, and L. Wichman (U.S. Fish and Wildlife Service); M. Abiouli, K. Clark, J. Miranda, A. Mueller, (California Department of Water Resources); C. Dale and D. Rocheleau (Natural Resource Scientists, Inc.); M. Archer (MBK Engineers); T. Ford and W. Monier (Modesto and Turlock Irrigation Districts); T. Stephens (Merced Irrigation District); S. Boyd (East Bay Municipal Utility District); E. Fuller, J. Inman, J. Pombo, and C. Sonke (FishBio Environmental); F. Bajjaliya, T. Devoe, C. Hanson, J. Karkanen, K. Karkanen, T. Musco (Hanson Environmental, Inc.); I. Werner (UC Davis); B. Herbold (U.S. Environmental Protection Agency;) L. Ploss and D. Westcot (San Joaquin River Group Authority); B. Bridges, L. Kiteck, S. Moore, and B. Wu (U.S. Bureau of Reclamation); J. Stuart (NOAA National Marine Fisheries Service); B. Anderson, M. Cozart, D. Gates, T. Heyne, S. Hoover, G. Litynksy, S. McCulloch, M. Serr, C. Sinclair, B. Smith, D. Thatcher, S. Tsao, L. Yamaguchi (California Department of Fish and Game); S. Borglin, R. Burks, J. Graham, J. Hanlon, K. Nyugen, C. Spier, and W. Stringfellow (University of Pacific); C. Battenfeld, J. George, T. Guerrero, and P. Stumpner, (USGS California Water Science Center); S. Brewer, J. Charrier, L. Gee, A. Grote, J. Plumb, M. Sholtis, and N. Swyers (USGS Columbia River Research Laboratory).

References Cited

Adams, N.S., Rondorf, D.W., Evans, S.D., and Kelly, J.E., 1998, Effects of surgically and gastrically implanted radio tags on growth and feeding behavior of juvenile Chinook salmon: Transactions of the American Fisheries Society, v.127, p. 128-136.

Adams, N.S., Plumb, J.M., Hatton, T.W., Jones, E.C., Swyers, N.M., Sholtis, M.D., Reagan, R.E., and Cash, K.M., 2008, Survival and migration behavior of juvenile salmonids at McNary Dam, 2006: Report to U.S. Army Corps of Engineers, Contract No. W68SBV60478899, Walla Walla Washington.

Adams, N.S., and Counihan, T.D., editors, 2009, Survival and migration behavior of juvenile salmonids at McNary Dam, 2007: Report to U.S. Army Corps of Engineers, Contract No. W68SBV70178419, Walla Walla, Washington.

Baker, P.F., Speed, T.P., and Ligon, F.K., 1995, Estimating the influence of temperature on survival of Chinook salmon smolts (*Oncorhynchus tshawytscha*) migrating through the Sacramento-San Joaquin Delta of California: Canadian Journal of Fisheries and Aquatic Sciences, v. 52, p. 855-863.

Burnham, K.P., Anderson, D.R., White, G.C., Brownie, C., and Pollock, K.H., 1987, Design and analysis methods for fish survival experiments based on release-recapture: American Fisheries Society, Monograph 5, Bethesda, Maryland.

Burnham, K.P., and Anderson, D.R., 2002, Model selection and multimodel inference: A practical information-theoretic approach, 2nd edition: Springer, New York, 488 p.

Brandes, P.L., and McLain, J.S., 2001, Juvenile Chinook salmon abundance, distribution, and survival in the Sacramento-San Joaquin Estuary, *in* Brown, R.L., ed., Contributions to the biology of Central Valley salmonids, v. 2, Fish Bulletin 179: California Department of Fish and Game, Sacramento, California, p. 39-138

Brownie, C., Hines, J.E., Nichols, J.D., Pollock, K.H, and Hestbeck, J.B., 1993, Capture-recapture studies for multiple strata including non-Markovian transitions: Biometrics, v. 49, p. 1173-1187.

Clark, G.H., 1929, Sacramento-San Joaquin salmon (*Oncorhynchus tschawytscha*) fishery of California: California Department of Fish and Game, Fisheries Bulletin No. 17, 73 p.

Cowan, L., and Schwarz, C.J., 2005, Capture-recapture studies using radio telemetry with premature radio-tag failure: Biometrics, v. 61, p. 657-664.

Ehrenberg, J.E., and Steig, T.W., 2003, Improved techniques for studying the temporal and spatial behaviour of a fish in a fixed location: ICES Journal of Marine Science, v. 60, p. 700-706.

Ferguson, H.W., 1981, The effects of water temperature on the development of proliferative kidney disease in rainbow trout, Salmo gairdneri: Journal of Fish Diseases, v. 4, p. 175-177.

Healey, M.C., Dettinger, M.D., and Norgaard, R.B., editors, 2008, The state of Bay-Delta science, 2008: CALFED Science Program, Sacramento, California, 174 p., available from < http://www.science.calwater.ca.gov/publications/>

Kimmerer, W.J., 2002, Physical, biological, and management responses to variable freshwater flow into the San Francisco Estuary: Estuaries, v. 25, p. 1275-1290.

Kimmerer, W.J., 2008, Losses of Sacramento River Chinook salmon and delta smelt to entrainment in water diversions in the Sacramento-San Joaquin Delta: San Francisco Estuary and Watershed Science, v. 6, p. 1-27.

Lady, J.M., Westhagen, P., and Skalski, J.R., 2008, USER 4: User specified estimation routine: University of Washington, available from <http://www.cbr.washington.edu/paramest/user/>

Lindley, S.T., Schick. R., May, B.P., Anderson, J.J., Greene, S., Hanson, C. Low, A., McEwan, D. MacFarlane, R. B., Swanson, C., and Williams, J.G., 2004, Population structure of threatened and endangered Chinook salmon ESUs in California's Central Valley Basin: National Marine Fisheries Service, La Jolla, California, Technical Memorandum no. 360, 56 p.

Lindley, S.T., Grimes, C.B., Mohr, M.S., Peterson, W., Stein, J., Anderson, J.T., Botsford, L.W., Bottom, D.L., Busack, C.A., Collier, T.K., Ferguson, J., Garza, J.C., Grover, A.M., Hankin, D.G., Kope, R.G., Lawson, P.W., Low, A., MacFarlane, R.B., Moore, K., Palmer-Zwahlen, M. Schwing, F.B., Smith, J., Tracy, C., Webb, R., Wells, B.K., and Williams, T.H., 2009, What caused the Sacramento River fall Chinook stock collapse?: Pre-publication report to the Pacific Fishery Management Council, 57 p.

Marine, K.R., and Cech, J.J., Jr., 2004, Effects of high water temperatures on growth, smoltification, and predator avoidance in juvenile Sacramento River Chinook salmon: North American Journal of Fisheries Management, v. 24, p. 198-210.

Martinelli, T.L., Hansel, H.C., and Shively, R.S., 1998, Growth and physiological responses to surgical and gastric radio tag implantation techniques in subyearling Chinook salmon: Hydrobiologia, v. 371/372, p. 79-87.

McCullagh, P., and Nelder, J., 1983, Generalized linear models: Chapman and Hall, London.

Myers, J.M., Kope, R.G., Bryant, G.J., Teel, D., Lierheimer, L.J., Wainwright, T.C., Grant, W.S., Waknitz, F.W., Neely, K., Lindley, S.T., and Waples, R.S., 1998, Status review of Chinook salmon from Washington, Idaho, Oregon, and California: National Marine Fisheries Service, La Jolla, California, Technical Memorandum no. 35, 443 p.

Newman, K.B., 2008, An evaluation of four Sacramento-San Joaquin River Delta juvenile salmon survival studies: U.S. Fish and Wildlife Service, Stockton, California, Project number SCI-06-299, available from <http://www.science.calwater.ca.gov/pdf/psp/>

Newman, K.B., and Rice, J., 2002, Modeling the survival of Chinook salmon smolts outmigrating through the lower Sacramento River system: Journal of the American Statistical Association, v. 97, p. 983-993.

Perry, R.W., Brandes, P.L., Sandstrom, P.T., Ammann, A., MacFarlane, B., Klimley, A.P., and Skalski, J.R., in press, Estimating survival and migration route probabilities of juvenile Chinook salmon in the Sacramento-San Joaquin River Delta: North American Journal of Fisheries Management.

Seber, G.A.F., 1982, The estimation of animal abundance and related parameters: Macmillan, New York.

San Joaquin River Group Authority, 2008, 2007 Technical Report: On implementing and monitoring of the San Joaquin River Agreement and the Vernalis Adaptive Management Plan: Prepared by San Joaquin River Group Authority for California Water Resource Control Board, 127 p.

San Joaquin River Group Authority, 2009, 2008 Technical Report: On implementing and monitoring of the San Joaquin River Agreement and the Vernalis Adaptive Management Plan: Prepared by San Joaquin River Group Authority for California Water Resource Control Board, 128 p.

Skalski, J.R., Townsend, R., Lady, J., Giorgi, A.E., Stevenson, J.R., and McDonald, R.S., 2002, Estimating route-specific passage and survival probabilities at a hydroelectric project from smolt radiotelemetry studies: Canadian Journal of Fisheries and Aquatic Sciences, v. 59, p. 1385-1393.

Skinner, J.E., 1962, An historical review of the fish and wildlife resources of the San Francisco Bay Area: California Department of Fish and Game, Sacramento, California, Water Projects Report no. 1, 226 p., available from <http://www.estuaryarchive.org/archive>

Smith, S.G., Muir, W.D., Hockersmith, E.E., Zabel, R.W., Graves, R.J., Ross, C.V., Connor, W.P., and Arnsberg, B.D., 2003, Influence of river conditions on survival and travel time of Snake River subyearling fall Chinook salmon: North American Journal of Fisheries Management, v. 23, p. 939-961.

The Bay Institute, 2003, The Bay Institute Ecological Scorecard: San Francisco Bay Index, 2003: The Bay Institute of San Francisco, 102 p., available from <http://www.bay.org/>

Townsend, R.L., Skalski, J.R., Dillingham, P., and Steig, T.W., 2006, Correcting bias in survival estimation resulting from tag failure in acoustic and radiotelemetry studies: Journal of Agricultural, Biological, and Environmental Statistics, v. 11, p. 1-14.

Wilder, R.M., and Ingram, J.F., 2006, Temporal patterns in catch rates of juvenile Chinook salmon and trawl net efficiencies in the Lower Sacramento River: IEP Newsletter, v. 19, p. 18-28.

Williams, J.G., 2006, Central Valley salmon: A perspective on Chinook and steelhead in the Central Valley of California: San Francisco Estuary and Watershed Science, v. 4, p. 1-398.

Yoshiyama, R.M., Fisher, F.W., and Moyle, P.B., 1998, Historical abundance and decline of Chinook salmon in the Central Valley region of California: North American Journal of Fisheries Management, v. 18, p. 487-521.

Appendix A. Parameter definitions and estimates

Table A1. Definitions of parameters in the release-recapture model.

Parameter	Definition
$S_{a0,DF}$	Tag survival probability between implantation and release at Durham Ferry
$S_{a0,ST}$	Tag survival probability between implantation and release at Stockton
σ_{a1}	Combined probability of fish survival and tag survival from release at Durham Ferry to SJO(s)
σ_{a2}	Joint probability of fish survival and tag survival from SJO.s to SJO(n),OLD
σ_{a3}	Joint probability of fish survival and tag survival from SJO.n to STP.s
σ_{a4}	Joint probability of fish survival and tag survival from STP.s to STP.n
$\sigma_{a5,DF}$	Joint probability of fish survival and tag survival from STP.n to SJT, TRN
$\sigma_{a5,ST}$	Joint probability of fish survival and tag survival from release at Stockton to SJT, TRN
σ_{a6}	Joint probability of fish survival and tag survival from SJT to any of the next monitoring sites at TMS, JPT, CCFB, or CVP
σ_{a7}	Joint probability of fish survival and tag survival from JPT to MAL
σ_{b1}	Joint probability of fish survival and tag survival from OLD to any of the next monitoring sites at TMS, JPT, CCFB, or CVP
σ_{b2}	Joint probability of fish survival and tag survival from CCFB to SWP
σ_{b3}	Joint probability of fish survival and tag survival from SWP to MAL
σ_{c1}	Joint probability of fish survival and tag survival from TRN to any of the next monitoring sites at TMS, JPT, CCFB, or CVP
σ_{d1}	Joint probability of fish survival and tag survival from CVP to MAL
σ_{e1}	Joint probability of fish survival and tag survival from TMS to MAL
Ψ_{a1}	Probability of remaining in the San Joaquin River (i.e., passing site SJO.n) at the Old River-San Joaquin River junction; equivalent to $(1 - \Psi_{b1})$
Ψ_{b1}	Probability of moving from the San Joaquin River into Old River (i.e., passing site OLD) at the Old River-San Joaquin River junction; equivalent to $(1 - \Psi_{a1})$
Ψ_{a2}	Probability of remaining in the San Joaquin River (i.e., passing SJT) at the Turner Cut-San Joaquin River junction; equivalent to $(1 - \Psi_{c2})$
Ψ_{c2}	Probability of moving from the San Joaquin River into Turner Cut (i.e., passing TRN) at the Turner Cut-San Joaquin River junction; equivalent to $(1 - \Psi_{a2})$
$\varphi_{a6,a7}$	Probability of moving from SJT toward JPT and surviving from SJT to JPT
$\varphi_{a6,b2}$	Probability of moving from SJT toward CCFB and surviving from SJT to CCFB
$\varphi_{a6,d1}$	Probability of moving from SJT toward CVP and surviving from SJT to CVP
$\varphi_{a6,e1}$	Probability of moving from SJT toward TMS and surviving from SJT to TMS
$\varphi_{b1,a7}$	Probability of moving from OLD toward JPT and surviving from OLD to JPT
$\varphi_{b1,b2}$	Probability of moving from OLD toward CCFB and surviving from OLD to CCFB
$\varphi_{b1,d1}$	Probability of moving from OLD toward CVP and surviving from OLD to CVP
$\varphi_{b1,e1}$	Probability of moving from OLD toward TMS and surviving from OLD to TMS
$\varphi_{c1,a7}$	Probability of moving from TRN toward JPT and surviving from TRN to JPT
$\varphi_{c1,b2}$	Probability of moving from TRN toward CCFB and surviving from TRN to CCFB
$\varphi_{c1,d1}$	Probability of moving from TRN toward CVP and surviving from TRN to CVP
$\varphi_{c1,e1}$	Probability of moving from TRN toward TMS and surviving from TRN to TMS
$P_{a1,DF}$	Detection probability in holding tanks at Merced River Hatchery during the 1 hr prior to departure from hatchery for fish released at Durham Ferry
$P_{a1,ST}$	Detection probability in holding tanks at Merced River Hatchery during the 1 hr prior to departure from hatchery for fish released at Stockton
P_{a2}	Detection probability at SJO.s
P_{a3}	Detection probability at SJO.n
P_{a4}	Detection probability at STP.s
P_{a5}	Detection probability at STP.n

Table A1. Continued.

Parameter	Definition
P_{a6}	Detection probability at SJT
$P_{a7,DF}$	Detection probability at JPT for fish released at Durham Ferry
$P_{a7,ST}$	Detection probability at JPT for fish released at Stockton
$P_{a8,DF}$	Detection probability at MAL for fish released at Durham Ferry
$P_{a8,ST}$	Detection probability at MAL for fish released at Stockton
P_{b1}	Detection probability at OLD
$P_{b2,DF}$	Detection probability at CCFB for fish released at Durham Ferry
$P_{b2,ST}$	Detection probability at CCFB for fish released at Stockton
P_{b3}	Detection probability at SWP
P_{c1}	Detection probability at TRN
P_{d1}	Detection probability at CVP
P_{e1}	Detection probability at TMS

Table A2. Parameter estimates (standard error in parentheses) with 95-percent profile likelihood confidence intervals (C.I.) for tagged juvenile Chinook salmon released during weeks 1 and 2.

[Parameters without standard errors or confidence intervals were set to fixed values in the model]

Parameter	Week 1 Estimate (SE)	Week 1 95% C. I.	Week 2 Estimate (SE)	Week 2 95% C. I.
$S_{a0,DF}$	0.86 (0.02)	0.82, 0.90	0.92 (0.02)	0.88, 0.95
$S_{a0,ST}$	0.86 (0.03)	0.81, 0.91	0.95 (0.02)	0.91, 1.00
σ_{a1}	0.92 (0.05)	0.82, 1.00	0.86 (0.02)	0.82, 0.90
σ_{a2}	0.85 (0.07)	0.72, 0.99	0.96 (0.02)	0.92, 1.00
σ_{a3}	0.85 (0.05)	0.75, 0.93	0.70 (0.05)	0.59, 0.79
σ_{a4}	0.96 (0.03)	0.87, 0.99	0.89 (0.05)	0.78, 0.98
$\sigma_{a5,DF}$	0.49 (0.07)	0.35, 0.63	0.56 (0.07)	0.42, 0.70
$\sigma_{a5,ST}$	0.52 (0.04)	0.44, 0.60	0.64 (0.04)	0.56, 0.71
σ_{a6}	0.51 (0.08)	0.37, 0.68	0.44 (0.05)	0.34, 0.54
σ_{a7}	0.61 (0.11)	0.40, 0.81	0.71 (0.08)	0.55, 0.84
σ_{b1}	0.62 (0.07)	0.51, 0.80	0.51 (0.05)	0.41, 0.62
σ_{b2}	0.37 (0.09)	0.21, 0.56	0.39 (0.10)	0.21, 0.59
σ_{b3}	0.16 (0.10)	0.03, 0.42	0.46 (0.15)	0.20, 0.75
σ_{c1}	0.03 (0.03)	0.00, 0.12	0.00	
σ_{d1}	0.11 (0.05)	0.04, 0.22	0.05 (0.04)	0.01, 0.15
σ_{e1}	0.52 (0.37)	0.04, 1.00	1.00	
Ψ_{a1}	0.32 (0.04)	0.25, 0.40	0.37 (0.03)	0.31, 0.44
Ψ_{b1}	0.68 (0.04)	0.60, 0.75	0.63 (0.03)	0.56, 0.69
Ψ_{a2}	0.68 (0.05)	0.58, 0.76	0.89 (0.03)	0.83, 0.94
Ψ_{c2}	0.32 (0.05)	0.24, 0.42	0.11 (0.03)	0.06, 0.17
$\varphi_{a6,a7}$	0.48 (0.08)	0.34, 0.65	0.40 (0.05)	0.31, 0.50
$\varphi_{a6,b2}$	0.00		0.00	
$\varphi_{a6,d1}$	0.00		0.00	
$\varphi_{a6,e1}$	0.03 (0.02)	0.00, 0.08	0.04 (0.02)	0.01, 0.08
$\varphi_{b1,a7}$	0.01 (0.01)	0.00, 0.04	0.01 (0.01)	0.00, 0.03
$\varphi_{b1,b2}$	0.27 (0.06)	0.18, 0.41	0.21 (0.04)	0.14, 0.32
$\varphi_{b1,d1}$	0.37 (0.05)	0.27, 0.47	0.29 (0.04)	0.22, 0.37
$\varphi_{b1,e1}$	0.00		0.00	
$\varphi_{c1,a7}$	0.00		0.00	

Table A2. Continued.

Parameter	Week 1 Estimate (SE)	Week 1 95% C. I.	Week 2 Estimate (SE)	Week 2 95% C. I.
$\varphi_{c1,b2}$	0.00		0.00	
$\varphi_{c1,d1}$	0.03 (0.03)	0.00, 0.12	0.00	
$\varphi_{c1,e1}$	0.00		0.00	
$P_{a1,DF}$	1.00		1.00	
$P_{a1,ST}$	1.00		1.00	
P_{a2}	0.36 (0.04)	0.29, 0.44	0.99 (0.01)	0.96, 1.00
P_{a3}	0.98 (0.02)	0.92, 1.00	0.98 (0.02)	0.92, 1.00
P_{a4}	0.92 (0.04)	0.82, 1.00	1.00	
P_{a5}	1.00		0.96 (0.04)	0.85, 1.00
P_{a6}	1.00		1.00	
$P_{a7,DF}$	0.67 (0.10)	0.45, 0.84	1.00	
$P_{a7,ST}$	$P_{a7,DF}$		0.77 (0.08)	0.59, 0.90
$P_{a8,DF}$	0.96 (0.03)	0.88, 1.00	0.98 (0.02)	0.91, 1.00
$P_{a8,ST}$	$P_{a8,DF}$		0.98 (0.02)	0.91, 1.00
P_{b1}	0.47 (0.06)	0.37, 0.58	0.94 (0.03)	0.86, 0.98
$P_{b2,DF}$	0.77 (0.12)	0.50, 0.94	0.82 (0.12)	0.54, 0.97
$P_{b2,ST}$	$P_{b2,DF}$		0.00	
P_{b3}	1.00		1.00	
P_{c1}	1.00		1.00	
P_{d1}	1.00		1.00	
P_{e1}	1.00		1.00